323.
Proctor, Robert, author.
Citizenship basics 2017 : 100
questions in Spanish : U.S.
citizenship study guide

5.39

Citizenship Basics: 100 U.S. Citizenship Study

Take this 10 question pre-test

Civics portion of the United S

(Tome este pre-test de 10 preguntas para ver si usted esta listo para la parte de la educación cívica de la entrevista de naturalización de los Estados Unidos.) Remember, you need a *minimum of 6 correct answers to pass (Recuerda, necesitas un mínimo de 6 respuestas correctas para pasar).*

NO LONGER
PROPERTY OF
LONGMONT PUBLIC
LIBRARY

English	Spanish
1. What ocean is on the West Coast of the United States?	1. ¿Qué océano está en la costa oeste de los Estados Unidos?
2. What is the name of the Speaker of the House of Representatives now?	2. ¿Cómo se llama el Presidente actual de la Cámara de Representantes?
3. How many U.S. Senators are there?	3. ¿Cuántos senadores de los Estados Unidos hay?
4. What do we call the first ten amendments to the Constitution?	4. ¿Con qué nombre se conocen las primeras diez enmiendas a la Constitución?
5. Who wrote the Declaration of Independence?	5. ¿Quién escribió la Declaración de Independencia?

LONGMONT PUBLIC LIBRARY
LONGMONT, COLORADO

Pre-Test Continued

English	Spanish
6. When do we celebrate Independence Day?	6. ¿Cuándo celebramos el Día de la Independencia?
7. Where is the Statue of Liberty?	7. ¿Dónde está la Estatua de la Libertad?
8. What do we show loyalty to when we say the Pledge of Allegiance?	8. ¿Ante qué demostramos nuestra lealtad cuando decimos el Juramento de Lealtad (Pledge of Allegiance)?
9. How many justices are on the Supreme Court?	9. ¿Cuántos jueces hay en la Corte Suprema de Justicia?
10. What does the President's Cabinet do?	10. ¿Qué hace el Gabinete del Presidente?

Answers- Respuestas

1. Pacific (el océano Pacífico)   2. Paul Ryan   3. one hundred (100) (cien)   4. the Bill of Rights (la Carta de Derechos)   5. (Thomas) Jefferson   6. July 4 (el 4 de julio) 7. New York (Harbor) (el puerto de Nueva York) Liberty Island   8. the United States (los Estados Unidos) the flag (la bandera)   9. nine (nueve)   10. advises the President (asesora al Presidente)

LONGMONT PUBLIC LIBRARY
LONGMONT, COLORADO

This is what **Citizenship Basics: 100 Questions in Spanish - U.S. Citizenship Study Guide 2017** looks like.

English	Spanish
5. What do we call the first ten amendments to the Constitution?	5. ¿Con qué nombre se conocen las primeras diez enmiendas a la Constitución?
• **the Bill of Rights**	• **la Carta de Derechos**
6. What is one right or freedom from the First Amendment?*	6. ¿Cuál es un derecho o libertad que la Primera Enmienda garantiza?*
• **speech** • **religion** • **assembly** • **press** • **petition the government**	• **expresión** • **religión** • **reunión** • **prensa** • **peticionar al gobierno**
7. How many amendments does the Constitution have?	7. ¿Cuántas enmiendas tiene la Constitución?
• **twenty-seven (27)**	• **veintisiete (27)**
8. What did the Declaration of Independence do?	8. ¿Qué hizo la Declaración de Independencia?

Preguntas de educación cívica del Examen de Naturalización

A continuación encontrara 100 preguntas y respuestas de educación cívica (historia y gobierno) del Examen de Naturalización. El examen de educación cívica es un examen oral durante el cual el oficial de USCIS le hará 10 de estas 100 preguntas. El solicitante debe contestar correctamente 6 de las 10 preguntas para aprobar la sección de educación cívica del Examen de Naturalización.

Examen de Naturalización, algunas respuestas varían y pueden cambiar por motivo de elecciones o nombramientos. Los solicitantes deben tener conocimiento de las respuestas actuales a estas preguntas. Los solicitantes deben contestar estas preguntas con el nombre del oficial o funcionario que ha sido nombrado y que está sirviendo en el puesto al momento de su entrevista con USCIS. El oficial de USCIS no aceptará una respuesta equivocada.

from USCIS

Qué puede esperar en el examen real
El examen real de civismo NO es un examen de selección múltiple. En la entrevista de naturalización, un funcionario de USCIS le hará hasta 10 preguntas de la lista de 100 preguntas en inglés. Usted debe responder correctamente 6 de las 10 preguntas para aprobar el examen de civismo.
Ciertos solicitantes, por su edad y tiempo con estatus de residente permanente, están exentos del requisito del dominio del idioma inglés y pueden tomar el examen de civismo en el idioma de su elección.

from USCIS

This book contains the 100 questions from the U.S. Citizenship Test in English and Spanish. The questions and answers are clearly presented in order to make learning easier.

Este libro contiene las 100 preguntas de la Prueba de Ciudadanía de los Estados Unidos en inglés y español.

Las preguntas y respuestas se presentan claramente para facilitar el aprendizaje.

About the Authors

Darin French

Darin has taught U.S. History, Government, Basic Language Arts, ESL and ESL/Citizenship for the Los Angeles Unified School District since 2007. He has also served as a CBET coordinator, ESL teacher advisor, and participated on several textbook selection committees and WASC accreditation teams. He received his BA in History and Political Science from the University of California at Los Angeles. Darin and Robert, together, have assisted hundreds of people in passing their U.S. naturalization tests.

Robert Proctor

Robert has taught citizenship and English as a Second Language classes in Los Angeles since 1996 and has helped hundreds of immigrants to pass their U.S. citizenship interviews. He is the co-author of several citizenship and ESL textbooks which are used by school districts, citizenship programs, and students across the United States. Robert regularly gives presentations at ESL/Citizenship conferences and workshops. Mr. Proctor received his degree from the University of California at Santa Barbara is a credentialed ESL and Citizenship Instructor for the Los Angeles Unified School District.

© 2017 Southern California Educational Services, LLC

ALL RIGHTS RESERVED. No part of this work covered by the copyright herein may be reproduced, transmitted, stored or used in any form or by any means graphic, electronic, or mechanical, including but not limited to photocopying, recording, scanning, digitizing, taping, Web distribution, information networks, or information storage and retrieval systems, except as permitted under Section 107 or 108 of the 1976 United States Copyright Act, without prior written permission of the publisher.

> For permission to use material from this text or product, submit all requests to
> darin@sceduserv.com

Southern California Educational Services, LLC
4555 E. 3rd St #3B
Los Angeles, CA 90022

Also Available from This Seller:
English Basics: Your Guide to Prepositions

Citizenship Basics is not affiliated with USCIS or the U.S. Government. Citizenship Basics is only meant to be a study tool for students preparing for their U.S. naturalization interviews.

Finding the Answers to
"Answers Will Vary" Questions

There are **4** questions on the civics test that have answers that will vary depending on where you live, what state you live in, and what zip code you live in within your state.

20. Who is one of your state's U.S. Senators now?
23. Name your U.S. Representative.
43. Who is the Governor of your state now?
44. What is the capital of your state?

Here are the links to the official websites so that you can find the correct answers to your particular location of residence.

Your state's U.S. Senators:
http://www.senate.gov/states/#

Your state's U.S. Representative:
http://www.house.gov/representatives/find/

Your state's Governor:
https://www.usa.gov/state-governor

Your state's capital:
http://www.50states.com

The United States Naturalization Test

Passing the test:

An applicant passes the civics test if he or she provides a correct answer or provides an alternative phrasing of the correct answer for **six of the ten** questions.

Failing the test:

An applicant fails the civics test if he or she provides an incorrect answer or fails to respond to six out of the ten questions from the standardized test form.

Special Consideration - Questions with an *

A USCIS officer gives special consideration to an applicant who is 65 years of age or older and who has been living in the United States for periods totaling at least 20 years subsequent to a lawful admission for permanent residence. The age and time requirements must be met at the time of filing the naturalization application. An officer only asks questions from the three "65/20" test forms when administering the civics test to such applicants. The test forms only contain 20 specially designated civics questions from the usual list of 100 questions. These are the questions that have an asterisk *.

If an applicant fails any portion of the English test, the civics test, or all tests during the initial naturalization examination, USCIS will reschedule the applicant to appear for a second examination between 60 and 90 days after the first examination. *Don't worry, if you study consistently up until your first interview, you should not have a problem.*

English	Spanish
1. What is the supreme law of the land?	1. ¿Cuál es la ley suprema de la nación?
• **the Constitution**	• **la Constitución**
2. What does the Constitution do?	2. ¿Qué hace la Constitución?
• **sets up the government** • **defines the government** • **protects basic rights of Americans**	• **establece el gobierno** • **define el gobierno** • **protege los derechos básicos de los ciudadanos**
3. The idea of self-government is in the first three words of the Constitution. What are these words?	3. Las primeras tres palabras de la Constitución contienen la idea de la autodeterminación (de que el pueblo se gobierna a sí mismo). ¿Cuáles son estas palabras?
• **We the People**	• **Nosotros el Pueblo**
4. What is an amendment?	4. ¿Qué es una enmienda?
• **a change (to the Constitution)** • **an addition (to the Constitution)**	• **un cambio (a la Constitución)** • **una adición (a la Constitución)**

English	Spanish
5. What do we call the first ten amendments to the Constitution?	5.¿Con qué nombre se conocen las primeras diez enmiendas a la Constitución?
• **the Bill of Rights**	• **la Carta de Derechos**
6. What is one right or freedom from the First Amendment?*	6. ¿Cuál es un derecho o libertad que la Primera Enmienda garantiza?*
• **speech** • **religion** • **assembly** • **press** • **petition the government**	• **expresión** • **religión** • **reunión** • **prensa** • **peticionar al gobierno**
7. How many amendments does the Constitution have?	7.¿Cuántas enmiendas tiene la Constitución?
• **twenty-seven (27)**	• **veintisiete (27)**
8. What did the Declaration of Independence do?	8.¿Qué hizo la Declaración de Independencia?

English	Spanish
• announced our independence (from Great Britain)	• anunció nuestra independencia (de Gran Bretaña)
• declared our independence (from Great Britain)	• declaró nuestra independencia (de Gran Bretaña)
• said that the United States is free (from Great Britain)	• dijo que los Estados Unidos se independizó (de Gran Bretaña)

9. What are two rights in the Declaration of Independence?

9. ¿Cuáles son dos derechos en la Declaración de la Independencia?

- life
- liberty
- pursuit of happiness

- la vida
- la libertad
- la búsqueda de la felicidad

10. What is freedom of religion?

10. ¿En qué consiste la libertad de religión?

- **You can practice any religion, or not practice a religion.**

- **Se puede practicar cualquier religión o no tener ninguna.**

11. What is the economic system in the United States? *

11. ¿Cuál es el sistema económico de los Estados Unidos?*

English	Spanish
• capitalist economy • market economy	• economía capitalista • economía del mercado
12. What is the "rule of law"?	12. ¿En qué consiste el "estado de derecho" (ley y orden)?
• Everyone must follow the law. • Leaders must obey the law. • Government must obey the law. • No one is above the law.	• Todos deben obedecer la ley. • Los líderes deben obedecer la ley. • El gobierno debe obedecer la ley. • Nadie está por encima de la ley.
13. Name one branch or part of the government.*	13. Nombre una rama o parte del gobierno.*

• Congress
• legislative
• President
• executive
• the courts
• judicial
	• Congreso
	  Poder legislativo
	• Presidente
	  Poder ejecutivolos
	• tribunales
	• Poder judicial

English	Spanish
14. What stops one branch of government from becoming too powerful?	14. ¿Qué es lo que hace que una rama del gobierno no se vuelva demasiado poderosa?
• **checks and balances** • **separation of powers**	• **pesos y contrapesos** • **separación de poderes**
15. Who is in charge of the executive branch?	15.¿Quién está a cargo de la rama ejecutiva?
• **the President**	• **el Presidente**
16. Who makes federal laws?	16. ¿Quién crea las leyes federales?
• **Congress** • **Senate and House (of Representatives)** • **(U.S. or national) legislature**	• **el Congreso** • **el Senado y la Cámara (de Representantes)** • **la legislatura (nacional o de los Estados Unidos)**
17. What are the two parts of the U.S. Congress?*	17. ¿Cuáles son las dos partes que integran el Congreso de los Estados Unidos?*

English	Spanish
• **the Senate and House (of Representatives)**	• **el Senado y la Cámara (de Representantes)**
18. How many U.S. Senators are there?	18. ¿Cuántos senadores de los Estados Unidos hay?
• **one hundred (100)**	• **cien (100)**
19. We elect a U.S. Senator for how many years?	19. ¿De cuántos años es el término de elección de un senador de los Estados Unidos?
• **six (6)**	• **seis (6)**
20. Who is one of your state's U.S. Senators now?*	20. Nombre a uno de los senadores actuales del estado donde usted vive.*

MicHaEL BeNNET
CORY GARDENER

English	Spanish
• **Answers will vary. [District of Columbia residents and residents of U.S. territories should answer that D.C. (or the territory where the applicant lives) has no U.S. Senators.]**	• **Las respuestas variarán. [Los residentes del Distrito de Columbia y los territorios de los Estados Unidos deberán contestar que el D.C. (o territorio en donde vive el solicitante) no cuenta con Senadores a nivel nacional.]**
21. The House of Representatives has how many voting members?	21. ¿Cuántos miembros votantes tiene la Cámara de Representantes?
• **four hundred thirty-five (435)**	• **cuatrocientos treinta y cinco (435)**
22. We elect a U.S. Representative for how many years?	22. ¿De cuántos años es el término de elección de un representante de los Estados Unidos?
• **two (2)**	• **dos (2)**
23. Name your U.S. Representative.	23. Dé el nombre de su representante a nivel nacional.

JOE NEGUSE

English	Spanish
• **Answers will vary. [Residents of territories with nonvoting Delegates or Resident Commissioners may** • **provide the name of that Delegate or Commissioner. Also acceptable is any statement that the territory has no (voting) Representatives in Congress.]**	• **Las respuestas variarán. [Los residentes de territorios con delegados no votantes o los comisionados residentes pueden decir el nombre de dicho delegado o comisionado. Una respuesta que indica que el territorio no tiene representantes votantes en el Congreso también es aceptable.]**
24. Who does a U.S. Senator represent?	24. ¿A quiénes representa un senador de los Estados Unidos?
• **all people of the state**	• **todas las personas del estado**
25. Why do some states have more Representatives than other states?	25. ¿Por qué tienen algunos estados más representantes que otros?

English	Spanish
• (because of) the state's population • (because) they have more people • (because) some states have more people	• (debido a) la población del estado • (debido a que) tienen más gente • (debido a que) algunos estados tienen más gente
26. We elect a President for how many years?	26. ¿De cuántos años es el término de elección de un presidente?
• **four (4)**	• **cuatro (4)**
27. In what month do we vote for President?*	27.¿En qué mes votamos por un nuevo presidente?*
• **November**	• **Noviembre**
28. What is the name of the President of the United States now?*	28. ¿Cómo se llama el actual Presidente de los Estados Unidos?*
• **Donald Trump** • **Trump**	• **Donald Trump** • **Trump**
29. What is the name of the Vice President of the United States now?	29. ¿Cómo se llama el actual Vicepresidente de los Estados Unidos?

English	Spanish
• **Michael Pence** • **Mike Pence** • **Pence**	• **Michael Pence** • **Mike Pence** • **Pence**
30. If the President can no longer serve, who becomes President?	30. Si el Presidente ya no puede cumplir sus funciones, ¿quién se vuelve Presidente?
• **the Vice President**	• **el Vicepresidente**
31. If both the President and the Vice President can no longer serve, who becomes President?	31. Si tanto el Presidente como el Vicepresidente ya no pueden cumplir sus funciones, ¿quién se vuelve Presidente?
• **the Speaker of the House**	• **el Presidente de la Cámara de Representantes**
Who is the Commander in Chief of the military?	32. ¿Quién es el Comandante en Jefe de las Fuerzas Armadas?
• **the President**	• **el Presidente**
33. Who signs bills to become laws?	33. ¿Quién firma los proyectos de ley para convertirlos en ley?
• **the President**	• **el Presidente**

English	Spanish
34. Who vetoes bills?	34. ¿Quién veta los proyectos de ley?
• **the President**	• **el Presidente**
35. What does the President's Cabinet do?	35. ¿Qué hace el Gabinete del Presidente?
• **advises the President**	• **asesora al Presidente**
36. What are two Cabinet-level positions?	36. ¿Cuáles son dos puestos a nivel de gabinete?

English	Spanish
• Secretary of Agriculture	• Secretario de Agricultura
• Secretary of Commerce	• Secretario de Comercio
• Secretary of Defense	• Secretario de Defensa
• Secretary of Education	• Secretario de Educación
• Secretary of Energy	• Secretario de Energía
• Secretary of Health and Human Services	• Secretario de Salud y Servicios Humanos
• Secretary of Homeland Security	• Secretario de Seguridad Nacional
• Secretary of Housing and Urban Development	• Secretario de Vivienda y Desarrollo Urbano
• Secretary of the Interior	• Secretario del Interior
• Secretary of Labor	• Secretario del Trabajo
• Secretary of State	• Secretario de Estado
• Secretary of Transportation	• Secretario de Transporte
• Secretary of the Treasury	• Secretario del Tesoro
• Secretary of Veterans Affairs	• Secretario de Asuntos de Veteranos
• Attorney General	• Procurador General
• Vice President	• Vicepresidente
37. What does the judicial branch do?	37. ¿Qué hace la rama judicial?

English	Spanish
• reviews laws	• revisa las leyes
• explains laws	• explica las leyes
• resolves disputes (disagreements)	• resuelve disputas(desacuerdos)
• decides if a law goes against the Constitution	• decide si una ley va en contra de la Constitución
38. What is the highest court in the United States?	38. ¿Cuál es el tribunal más alto de los Estados Unidos?
• the Supreme Court	• la Corte Suprema de Justicia
39. How many justices are on the Supreme Court?	39. ¿Cuántos jueces hay en la Corte Suprema de Justicia?
• nine (9)	• nueve (9)
40. Who is the Chief Justice of the United States now?	40. ¿Quién es el Presidente actual de la Corte Suprema de Justicia de los Estados Unidos?
• John Roberts (John G. Roberts, Jr.)	• John Roberts (John G. Roberts, Jr.)

English	Spanish
41. Under our Constitution, some powers belong to the federal government. What is one power of the federal government?	41. De acuerdo a nuestra Constitución, algunos poderes pertenecen al gobierno federal. ¿Cuál es un poder del gobierno federal?

- **to print money**
- **to declare war**
- **to create an army**
- **to make treaties**

- **imprimir dinero**
- **declarar la guerra**
- **crear un ejército**
- **suscribir tratados**

English	Spanish
42. Under our Constitution, some powers belong to the states. What is one power of the states?	42. De acuerdo a nuestra Constitución, algunos poderes pertenecen a los estados. ¿Cuál es un poder de los estados?

- **provide schooling and education**
- **provide protection (police)**
- **provide safety (fire departments)**
- **give a driver's license**
- **approve zoning and land use**

- **proveer escuelas y educación**
- **proveer protección (policía)**
- **proveer seguridad (cuerpos de bomberos)**
- **conceder licencias de conducir**
- **aprobar la zonificación y uso de la tierra**

English	Spanish
43. Who is the Governor of your state now?	43. ¿Quién es el gobernador actual de su estado? *JARED POLIS*
• **Answers will vary. [District of Columbia residents should answer that D.C. does not have a Governor.]**	• **Las respuestas variarán. [Los residentes del Distrito de Columbia deben decir "no tenemos gobernador".]**
44. What is the capital of your state?*	44. ¿Cuál es la capital de su estado?* *Colorado*
• **Answers will vary. [District of Columbia residents should answer that D.C. is not a state and does not have a capital. Residents of U.S. territories should name the capital of the territory.]**	• **Las respuestas variarán. [Los residentes del Distrito de Columbia deben contestar que el D.C. no es estado y que no tiene capital. Los residentes de los territorios de los Estados Unidos deben dar el nombre de la capital del territorio.]**
45. What are the two major political parties in the United States?*	45. ¿Cuáles son los dos principales partidos políticos de los Estados Unidos?*
• **Democratic and Republican**	• **Demócrata y Republicano**

English	Spanish
46. What is the political party of the President now?	40. ¿Cuál es el partido político del Presidente actual?
• **Republican (Party)**	• **(Partido) Republicano**
47. What is the name of the Speaker of the House of Representatives now?	41. ¿Cómo se llama el Presidente actual de la Cámara de Representantes?
• **Paul Ryan**	• **Paul D. Ryan** • **(Paul) Ryan**
48. There are four amendments to the Constitution about who can vote. Describe one of them.	48. Existen cuatro enmiendas a la Constitución sobre quién puede votar. Describa una de ellas.

English	Spanish
• Citizens eighteen (18) and older (can vote). • You don't have to pay (a poll tax) to vote. • Any citizen can vote. (Women and men can vote.) • A male citizen of any race (can vote).	• Ciudadanos de dieciocho (18) años en adelante (pueden votar). • No se exige pagar un impuesto para votar (el impuesto para acudir a las urnas o "poll tax" en inglés). • Cualquier ciudadano puede votar. (Tanto las mujeres como los hombres pueden votar.) • Un hombre ciudadano de cualquier raza (puede votar).
49. What is one responsibility that is only for United States citizens?*	49. ¿Cuál es una responsabilidad que corresponde sólo a los ciudadanos de los Estados Unidos?*
• serve on a jury • vote in a federal election	• prestar servicio en un jurado • votar en una elección federal

English	Spanish
50. Name one right only for United States citizens.	50. ¿Cuál es un derecho que pueden ejercer sólo los ciudadanos de los Estados Unidos?
• **vote in a federal election** • **run for federal office**	• **votar en una elección federal** • **postularse a un cargo político federal**
51. What are two rights of everyone living in the United States?	51. ¿Cuáles son dos derechos que pueden ejercer todas las personas que viven en los Estados Unidos?
• **freedom of expression** • **freedom of speech** • **freedom of assembly** • **freedom to petition the government** • **freedom of worship** • **the right to bear arms**	• **libertad de expresión** • **libertad de la palabra** • **libertad de reunión** • **libertad para peticionar al gobierno** • **libertad de religión** • **el derecho a portar armas**
52. What do we show loyalty to when we say the Pledge of Allegiance?	52. ¿Ante qué demostramos nuestra lealtad cuando decimos el Juramento de Lealtad (Pledge of Allegiance)?

English	Spanish
• the United States	• los Estados Unidos
• the flag	• la bandera

53. What is one promise you make when you become a United States citizen?	53. ¿Cuál es una promesa que usted hace cuando se convierte en ciudadano de los Estados Unidos?

• give up loyalty to other countries	• renunciar la lealtad a otros países
• defend the Constitution and laws of the United States	• defender la Constitución y las leyes de los Estados Unidos
• obey the laws of the United States	• obedecer las leyes de los Estados Unidos
• serve in the U.S. military (if needed)	• prestar servicio en las Fuerzas Armadas de los Estados Unidos (de ser necesario)
• serve (do important work for) the nation (if needed)	• prestar servicio a (realizar trabajo importante para) la nación (de ser necesario)
• be loyal to the United States	• ser leal a los Estados Unidos

English	Spanish
54. How old do citizens have to be to vote for President?*	54. ¿Cuántos años tienen que tener los ciudadanos para votar por el Presidente? *
• **eighteen (18) and older**	• **dieciocho (18) años en adelante**
55. What are two ways that Americans can participate in their democracy?	55. ¿Cuáles son dos maneras mediante las cuales los ciudadanos americanos pueden participar en su democracia?

English	Spanish
• vote	• votar
• join a political party	• afiliarse a un partido político
• help with a campaign	• ayudar en una campaña
• join a civic group	• unirse a un grupo cívico
• join a community group	• unirse a un grupo comunitario
• give an elected official your opinion on an issue	• presentar su opinión sobre un asunto a un oficial elegido
• call Senators and Representatives	• llamar a los senadores y representantes
• publicly support or oppose an issue or policy	• apoyar u oponerse públicamente a un asunto o política
• run for office	• postularse a un cargo político
• write to a newspaper	• enviar una carta o mensaje a un periódico
56. When is the last day you can send in federal income tax forms?*	56. ¿Cuál es la fecha límite para enviar la declaración federal de impuesto sobre el ingreso?*
• April 15	• el 15 de abril

English	Spanish
57. When must all men register for the Selective Service?	57. ¿Cuándo deben inscribirse todos los hombres en el Servicio Selectivo?
• **at age eighteen (18)** • **between eighteen (18) and twenty-six (26)**	• **a la edad de dieciocho (18) años** • **entre los dieciocho (18) y veintiséis (26) años de edad**
58. What is one reason colonists came to America?	58. ¿Cuál es una razón por la que los colonos vinieron a los Estados Unidos?
• **freedom** • **political liberty** • **religious freedom** • **economic opportunity** • **practice their religion** • **escape persecution**	• **libertad** • **libertad política** • **libertad religiosa** • **oportunidad económica** • **para practicar su religión** • **para huir de la persecución**
59. Who lived in America before the Europeans arrived?	59. ¿Quiénes vivían en los Estados Unidos antes de la llegada de los europeos?
• **American Indians** • **Native Americans**	• **Indios americanos** • **Nativos americanos**

English	Spanish
60. What group of people was taken to America and sold as slaves?	60. ¿Qué pueblo fue traído a los Estados Unidos y vendido como esclavos?
<ul><li>**Africans**</li><li>**people from Africa**</li></ul>	<ul><li>**Africanos**</li><li>**gente de África**</li></ul>
61. Why did the colonists fight the British?	61. ¿Por qué lucharon los colonos contra los británicos?
<ul><li>**because of high taxes (taxation without representation)**</li><li>**because the British army stayed in their houses (boarding, quartering)**</li><li>**because they didn't have self-government**</li></ul>	<ul><li>**debido a los impuestos altos (impuestos sin representación)**</li><li>**el ejército británico se quedó en sus casas (alojamiento, acuartelamiento)**</li><li>**no tenían autodeterminación**</li></ul>
62. Who wrote the Declaration of Independence?	62. ¿Quién escribió la Declaración de Independencia?
<ul><li>**(Thomas) Jefferson**</li></ul>	<ul><li>**(Thomas) Jefferson**</li></ul>
63. When was the Declaration of Independence adopted?	63. ¿Cuándo fue adoptada la Declaración de Independencia?

English	Spanish
• July 4, 1776	• el 4 de julio de 1776
64. There were 13 original states. Name three.	64. Había 13 estados originales. Nombre tres.
• New Hampshire • Massachusetts • Rhode Island • Connecticut • New York • New Jersey • Pennsylvania • Delaware • Maryland • Virginia • North Carolina • South Carolina • Georgia	• Nueva Hampshire • Massachusetts • Rhode Island • Connecticut • Nueva York • Nueva Jersey • Pennsylvania • Delaware • Maryland • Virginia • Carolina del Norte • Carolina del Sur • Georgia
65. What happened at the Constitutional Convention?	65. ¿Qué ocurrió en la Convención Constitucional?

English	Spanish
• **The Constitution was written.** • **The Founding Fathers wrote the Constitution.**	• **Se redactó la Constitución.** • **Los Padres Fundadores redactaron la Constitución.**
66. When was the Constitution written?	66. ¿Cuándo fue escrita la Constitución?
• **1787**	• **1787**
67. The Federalist Papers supported the passage of the U.S. Constitution. Name one of the writers.	67. Los ensayos conocidos como "Los Federalistas" respaldaron la aprobación de la Constitución de los Estados Unidos. Nombre uno de los autores.
• **(James) Madison** • **(Alexander) Hamilton** • **(John) Jay** • **Publius**	• **(James) Madison** • **(Alexander) Hamilton** • **(John) Jay** • **Publius**
68. What is one thing Benjamin Franklin is famous for?	68. Mencione una razón por la que es famoso Benjamin Franklin.

English	Spanish
- U.S. diplomat - oldest member of the Constitutional Convention - first Postmaster General of the United States - writer of "Poor Richard's Almanac" - started the first free libraries	- diplomático americano - el miembro de mayor edad de la Convención Constitucional - primer Director General de Correos de los Estados Unidos - autor de "Poor Richard's Almanac" (Almanaque del Pobre Richard) - undó las primeras bibliotecas gratuitas
69. Who is the "Father of Our Country"?	69. ¿Quién se conoce como el "Padre de Nuestra Nación"?
- (George) Washington	- (George) Washington
70. Who was the first President?*	70. ¿Quién fue el primer Presidente?*
- (George) Washington	- (George) Washington

English	Spanish
71. What territory did the United States buy from France in 1803?	71. ¿Qué territorio compró los Estados Unidos de Francia en 1803?
• **the Louisiana Territory** • **Louisiana**	• **el territorio de Louisiana** • **Louisiana**
72. Name one war fought by the United States in the 1800s.	72. Mencione una guerra durante los años 1800 en la que peleó los Estados Unidos.
• **War of 1812** • **Mexican-American War** • **Civil War** • **Spanish-American War**	• **la Guerra de 1812** • **la Guerra entre México y los Estados Unidos** • **la Guerra Civil** • **la Guerra Hispanoamericana**
73. Name the U.S. war between the North and the South.	73. Dé el nombre de la guerra entre el Norte y el Sur de los Estados Unidos.
• **the Civil War** • **the War between the States**	• **la Guerra Civil** • **la Guerra entre los Estados**

English	Spanish
74. Name one problem that led to the Civil War.	74. Mencione un problema que condujo a la Guerra Civil.
• **slavery** • **economic reasons** • **states' rights**	• **esclavitud** • **razones económicas** • **derechos de los estados**
75. What was one important thing that Abraham Lincoln did?*	75. ¿Qué fue una cosa importante que hizo Abraham Lincoln?*
• **freed the slaves (Emancipation Proclamation)** • **saved (or preserved) the Union** • **led the United States during the Civil War**	• **liberó a los esclavos (Proclamación de la Emancipación)** • **salvó (o preservó) la Unión** • **presidió los Estados Unidos durante la Guerra Civil**
76. What did the Emancipation Proclamation do?	76. ¿Qué hizo la Proclamación de la Emancipación?

English	Spanish
• freed the slaves • freed slaves in the Confederacy • freed slaves in the Confederate states • freed slaves in most Southern states	• liberó a los esclavos • liberó a los esclavos de la Confederación • liberó a los esclavos en los estados de la Confederación • liberó a los esclavos en la mayoría de los estados del Sur
77. What did Susan B. Anthony do?	77. ¿Qué hizo Susan B. Anthony?
• fought for women's rights • fought for civil rights	• luchó por los derechos de la mujer • luchó por los derechos civiles
78. Name one war fought by the United States in the 1900s.*	78. Mencione una guerra durante los años 1900 en la que peleó los Estados Unidos.*

English	Spanish
• World War I • World War II • Korean War • Vietnam War • (Persian) Gulf War	• la Primera Guerra Mundial • la Segunda Guerra Mundial • la Guerra de Corea • la Guerra de Vietnam • la Guerra del Golfo (Persa)
79. Who was President during World War I?	79. ¿Quién era presidente durante la Primera Guerra Mundial?
• (Woodrow) Wilson	• (Woodrow) Wilson
80. Who was President during the Great Depression and World War II?	80. ¿Quién era presidente durante la Gran Depresión y la Segunda Guerra Mundial?
• (Franklin) Roosevelt	• (Franklin) Roosevelt
81. Who did the United States fight in World War II?	81. ¿Contra qué países peleó los Estados Unidos en la Segunda Guerra Mundial?
• Japan, Germany, and Italy	• Japón, Alemania e Italia
82. Before he was President, Eisenhower was a general. What war was he in?	82. Antes de ser presidente, Eisenhower era general. ¿En qué guerra participó?

English	Spanish
• **World War II**	• **Segunda Guerra Mundial**
83. During the Cold War, what was the main concern of the United States?	83. Durante la Guerra Fría, ¿cuál era la principal preocupación de los Estados Unidos?
• **Communism**	• **Comunismo**
84. What movement tried to end racial discrimination?	84. ¿Qué movimiento trató de poner fin a la discriminación racial?
• **civil rights (movement)**	• **(el movimiento en pro de los) derechos civiles**
85. What did Martin Luther King, Jr. do?*	85. ¿Qué hizo Martin Luther King, Jr.?*
• **fought for civil rights** • **worked for equality for all Americans**	• **luchó por los derechos civiles** • **trabajó por la igualdad de todos los ciudadanos americanos**
86. What major event happened on September 11, 2001, in the United States?	86. ¿Qué suceso de gran magnitud ocurrió el 11 de septiembre de 2001 en los Estados Unidos?

English	Spanish
• **Terrorists attacked the United States.**	• **Los terroristas atacaron los Estados Unidos.**
87. Name one American Indian tribe in the United States. [USCIS Officers will be supplied with a list of federally recognized American Indian tribes.]	87. Mencione una tribu de indios americanos de los Estados Unidos.

English	Spanish
• Cherokee	• Cherokee
• Navajo	• Navajo
• Sioux	• Sioux
• Chippewa	• Chippewa
• Choctaw	• Choctaw
• Pueblo	• Pueblo
• Apache	• Apache
• Iroquois	• Iroquois
• Creek	• Creek
• Blackfeet	• Blackfeet
• Seminole	• Seminole
• Cheyenne	• Cheyenne
• Arawak	• Arawak
• Shawnee	• Shawnee
• Mohegan	• Mohegan
• Huron	• Huron
• Oneida	• Oneida
• Lakota	• Lakota
• Crow	• Crow
• Teton	• Teton
• Hopi	• Hopi
• Inuit	• Inuit

English	Spanish
88. Name one of the two longest rivers in the United States.	88. Mencione uno de los dos ríos más largos en los Estados Unidos.
• **Missouri (River)** • **Mississippi (River)**	• **(el río) Missouri** • **(el río) Mississippi**
89. What ocean is on the West Coast of the United States?	89. ¿Qué océano está en la costa oeste de los Estados Unidos?
• **Pacific (Ocean)**	• **(el océano) Pacífico**
90. What ocean is on the East Coast of the United States?	90. ¿Qué océano está en la costa este de los Estados Unidos?
• **Atlantic (Ocean)**	• **(el océano) Atlántico**
91. Name one U.S. territory.	91. Dé el nombre de un territorio de los Estados Unidos.
• **Puerto Rico** • **U.S. Virgin Islands** • **American Samoa** • **Northern Mariana Islands** • **Guam**	• **Puerto Rico** • **Islas Vírgenes de los Estados Unidos** • **Samoa Americana** • **Islas Marianas del Norte** • **Guam**

English	Spanish
92. Name one state that borders Canada.	92. Mencione un estado que tiene frontera con Canadá.

- **Maine**
- **New Hampshire**
- **Vermont**
- **New York**
- **Pennsylvania**
- **Ohio**
- **Michigan**
- **Minnesota**
- **North Dakota**
- **Montana**
- **Idaho**
- **Washington**
- **Alaska**

	Maine
	Nueva Hampshire
	Vermont
	Nueva York
	Pennsylvania
	Ohio
	Michigan
	Minnesota
	Dakota del Norte
	Montana
	Idaho
	Washington
	Alaska

93. Name one state that borders Mexico.	93. Mencione un estado que tiene frontera con México.

- **California**
- **Arizona**
- **New Mexico**
- **Texas**

- **California**
- **Arizona**
- **Nuevo México**
- **Texas**

94. What is the capital of the United States?*	94. ¿Cuál es la capital de los Estados Unidos?*

- **Washington, D.C.**

- **Washington, D.C.**

English	Spanish
95. Where is the Statue of Liberty?*	95. ¿Dónde está la Estatua de la Libertad?*
• **New York (Harbor)** • **Liberty Island** • **[Also acceptable are New Jersey, near New York City, and on the Hudson (River).]**	• **(el puerto de) Nueva York** • **Liberty Island** • **[Otras respuestas aceptables son Nueva Jersey, cerca de la Ciudad de Nueva York y (el río) Hudson.]**
96. Why does the flag have 13 stripes?	96. ¿Por qué hay 13 franjas en la bandera?
• **because there were 13 original colonies** • **because the stripes represent the original colonies**	• **porque representan las 13 colonias originales** • **porque las franjas representan las colonias originales**
97. Why does the flag have 50 stars?*	97. ¿Por qué hay 50 estrellas en la bandera?*
• **because there is one star for each state** • **because each star represents a state** • **because there are 50 states**	• **porque hay una estrella por cada estado** • **porque cada estrella representa un estado** • **porque hay 50 estados**

English	Spanish
98. What is the name of the national anthem?	98. ¿Cómo se llama el himno nacional?
• **The Star-Spangled Banner**	• **The Star-Spangled Banner**
99. When do we celebrate Independence Day?*	99. ¿Cuándo celebramos el Día de la Independencia?*
• **July 4**	• **el 4 de julio**
100. Name two national U.S. holidays.	100. Mencione dos días feriados nacionales de los Estados Unidos.
• **New Year's Day** • **Martin Luther King, Jr. Day** • **Presidents' Day** • **Memorial Day** • **Independence Day** • **Labor Day** • **Columbus Day** • **Veterans Day** • **Thanksgiving** • **Christmas**	• **el Día de Año Nuevo** • **el Día de Martin Luther King, Jr.** • **el Día de los Presidentes** • **el Día de la Recordación** • **el Día de la Independencia** • **el Día del Trabajo** • **el Día de la Raza (Cristóbal Colón)** • **el Día de los Veteranos** • **el Día de Acción de Gracias** • **el Día de Navidad**

CPSIA information can be obtained
at www.ICGtesting.com
Printed in the USA
LVOW10s2259270417

532508LV00008B/131/P

9 781542 579490